TREES

Trees

Trees

From mighty dense rainforests to palm-fringed tropical islands and from taiga forests of spruce and pine to deciduous woodlands in temperate areas, trees are an integral and vital part of life on Earth. They provide shade, regulate the temperature and produce the oxygen to help us breathe.

Trees come in so many forms, from the hundred-metre high sequoias of California to tiny bonsai trees in homes and gardens.

We are fascinated by the beauty of their blossom, feast on their bountiful fruit, and use their wood as building materials and fuel.

Over millennia trees have inspired humans to write and paint. This book is intended as a celebration of trees, combining beautiful watercolours and other artworks with quotes about trees, nature and life in general.

"When the oak is felled the whole forest echoes with its fall, but a hundred acorns are sown in silence by an unnoticed breeze."

– THOMAS CARLYLE

"The coming and going of the seasons give us more than the springtimes, summers, autumns, and winters of our lives. It reflects the coming and going of the circumstances of our lives like the glassy surface of a pond that shows our faces radiant with joy or contorted with pain."

– GARY ZUKAV

"If it were possible to cure evils by lamentation and to raise the dead with tears, then gold would be a less valuable thing than weeping."

– SOPHOCLES

"*The clearest way into the Universe is through a forest wilderness.*"

– JOHN MUIR

"*In a good play every speech should be as fully flavoured as a nut or apple.*"

– JOHN MILLINGTON SYNGE

"In October, a maple tree before your window lights up your room like a great lamp. Even on cloudy days, its presence helps to dispel the gloom."

– JOHN BURROUGHS

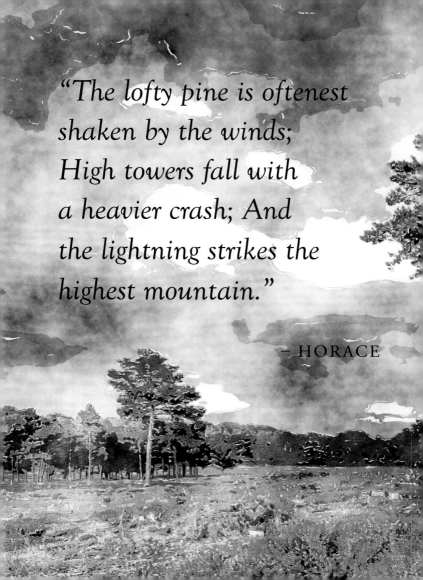

"The lofty pine is oftenest
shaken by the winds;
High towers fall with
a heavier crash; And
the lightning strikes the
highest mountain."

– HORACE

"*Old age is like everything else. To make a success of it, you've got to start young.*"

– THEODORE ROOSEVELT

"*This continent,
an open palm spread
frank before the sky.*"

– JAMES AGEE

"*Time will pass and seasons will come and go.*"

– ROY BEAN

"I can't be expected
to produce deathless
prose in an atmosphere
of gloom and eucalyptus."

– GERALD DURRELL

*"It is sad to grow old
but nice to ripen."*

– BRIGITTE BARDOT

"Sameness is the mother of disgust, variety the cure."

– PETRARCH

"*The ginkgo tree is from the era of dinosaurs, but while the dinosaur has been extinguished, the modern ginkgo has not changed. After the atomic bomb in Hiroshima, the ginkgo was the first tree that came up. It's amazing.*"

– KOJI NAKANISHI

*"Friendship is
a sheltering tree."*

– SAMUEL TAYLOR COLERIDGE

"*Autumn is a second spring when every leaf is a flower.*"

– ALBERT CAMUS

"To me a lush carpet of pine needles or spongy grass is more welcome than the most luxurious Persian rug."

– HELEN KELLER

"*You are like a chestnut burr, prickly outside, but silky-soft within, and a sweet kernel, if one can only get at it. Love will make you show your heart some day, and then the rough burr will fall off.*"

– LOUISA MAY ALCOTT

"*Be eccentric now. Don't wait for old age to wear purple.*"

– REGINA BRETT

"You can't stay in your corner
of the forest waiting for others
to come to you. You have to
go to them sometimes."

– A.A. MILNE

"*The olive tree is a tree full of health. It is a symbol of eternity. Of all things, it has peace attached to it.*"

– CAROL DRINKWATER

"Better than any argument
is to rise at dawn and pick
dew-wet red berries in a cup."

– WENDELL BERRY

"*Wisdom is like
a baobab tree;
no one individual
can embrace it.*"

– AFRICAN PROVERB

"*Remember, the storm is a good opportunity for the pine and the cypress to show their strength and their stability.*"

– HO CHÍ MINH

"I'd like to divide myself in order to see, among these mountains, each and every flower of every cherry tree."

– SAIGYŌ

"*The ordinary chestnut can beget a sickly and reluctant laugh, but it takes a horse chestnut to fetch the gorgeous big horse-laugh.*"

– MARK TWAIN

"*The birch trees loom ahead like a brotherhood of ghosts.*"

– LISA ANN SANDELL

"It is true, as they say, that the blossoms of spring are all the more precious because they bloom so briefly."

– MURASAKI SHIKIBU

"*Every particular in nature,
a leaf, a drop, a crystal,
a moment of time is related
to the whole, and partakes of
the perfection of the whole.*"

– RALPH WALDO EMERSON

"I would be a kapok tree
by your side
Standing with you
both of us shaped like trees.
Our roots hold hands
underground,
Our leaves touch
in the clouds."

– SHU TING

"A man watches his pear-tree day after day, impatient for the ripening of the fruit. Let him attempt to force the process, and he may spoil both fruit and tree. But let him patiently wait, and the ripe pear at length falls into his lap."

– ABRAHAM LINCOLN

"*I must have flowers,
always and always.*"

– CLAUDE MONET

"*The evergreen! How beautiful, how welcome, how wonderful the evergreen! When one thinks of it, how astonishing a variety of nature!*"

– JANE AUSTEN

"*Life without love is like a tree without blossoms or fruit.*"

– KHALIL GIBRAN

"No sun outlasts its sunset
but will rise again and
bring the dawn."

– MAYA ANGELOU

"I am a forest, and a night of dark trees: but he who is not afraid of my darkness, will find banks full of roses under my cypresses."

– FRIEDRICH NIETZSCHE

"*Delicious autumn!*
My very soul is wedded to it,
and if I were a bird I would
fly about the earth seeking
the successive autumns."

– GEORGE ELIOT

"Notice that the stiffest tree is most easily cracked, while the bamboo or willow survives by bending with the wind."

– BRUCE LEE

"*Almond blossom, sent to teach us that the spring days soon will reach us.*"

– EDWIN ARNOLD

"*Australians were unique due to our corals, our apples, our gum trees and our kangaroos.*"

– HAROLD HOLT

"*Our brains are like bonsai trees, growing around our private versions of reality.*"

– SLOANE CROSLEY

"*My silks and fine array, my smiles and languished air, by love are driv'n away. And mournful lean despair brings me yew to deck my grave: Such end true lovers have.*"

– WILLIAM BLAKE

"*The best time to plant a tree was twenty-five years ago. The second-best time to plant a tree is today.*"

– ELIUD KIPCHOGE

"An apple is an
excellent thing – until
you have tried a peach."

– GEORGE DU MAURIER

"*I remember a hundred lovely lakes, and recall the fragrant breath of pine and fir and cedar and poplar trees. The trail has strung upon it, as upon a thread of silk, opalescent dawns and saffron sunsets.*"

– HAMLIN GARLAND

"In every change, in every falling leaf there is some pain, some beauty. And that's the way new leaves grow."

– AMIT RAY

"*There is much to be said for cherry blossoms, but they seem so flighty. They are so quick to run off and leave you.*"

– MURASAKI SHIKIBU

"*People don't notice whether it's winter or summer when they're happy.*"

– ANTON CHEKHOV

"*The ego is like the root of a banyan tree, you think you have removed it all then one fine morning you see a sprout flourishing again.*"

– RAMAKRISHNA

"I draw flowers every day and send them to my friends so they get fresh blooms every morning."

– DAVID HOCKNEY

"No greater thing is created suddenly, any more than a bunch of grapes or a fig. If you tell me that you desire a fig, I answer you that there must be time. Let it first blossom, then bear fruit, then ripen."

– EPICTETUS

"If you tell a joke in the forest, but nobody laughs, was it a joke?"

– STEVEN WRIGHT

"*Fragrant o'er all the western groves, the tall magnolia towers unshaded.*"

– MARIA GOWEN BROOKS

"To climb in the canopy
I must leave the ground.
And such a decision will
determine whether I will live
a life of forest vistas, or an
existence of dirt and leaves."

– CRAIG D. LOUNSBROUGH

"By depending on the great,
the small may rise high.
See: the little plant ascending
the tall tree has climbed
to the top."

– SAKYA PANDITA

"I was for a while troubled with the haunting fear that if I handled the flower freely its bloom would fade – the sweet charm of freshness would leave it. I did not know then that it was no transitory blossom, but rather the radiant resemblance of one, cut in an indestructible gem."

– CHARLOTTE BRONTË

"*Autumn ... the year's last, loveliest smile.*"

– JOHN HOWARD BRYANT

"We ought to think that we are one of the leaves of a tree, and the tree is all humanity. We cannot live without the others, without the tree."

– PABLO CASALS

"*Every acorn on the ground
is just as alive as the three-
hundred-year-old oak tree that
towers over it.*"

– HOPE JAHREN

"See a flame in a spark,
a tree in a seed. See great
things in little beginnings."

– RICHARD SIBBES

"*The Poplar grows up straight and tall, The Pear-tree spreads along the wall.*"

— SARA COLERIDGE

Published in 2024 by Reed New Holland Publishers
Sydney

Level 1, 178 Fox Valley Road, Wahroonga, NSW 2076, Australia

newhollandpublishers.com

A record of this book is held at the National Library of Australia.

ISBN 9781921073632

Managing Director: Fiona Schultz
Publisher and Project Editor: Simon Papps
Designer: Andrew Davies
Production Director: Arlene Gippert
Printed in China

10 9 8 7 6 5 4 3 2 1

OTHER TITLES BY REED NEW HOLLAND INCLUDE:

A Field Guide to Australian Trees (Third Edition)
Ivan Holliday
ISBN 978 1 87633 479 6

A Guide to Flowers and Plants of Tasmania (Sixth Edition)
Launceston Field Naturalists Club
ISBN 978 1 92554 692 7

Australian Native Plants (Seventh Edition)
John W. Wrigley and Murray Fagg
ISBN 978 1 92554 691 0

Native Plants of Northern Australia (New Edition)
John Brock
ISBN 978 1 92554 682 8

Reed Concise Guide: Trees of Australia
David L. Jones
ISBN 978 1 92554 688 0

The Practical Gardener's Guide to Trees, Shrubs and Climbers
Stephanie Jackson
ISBN 978 1 76079 442 2

For details of these books and hundreds of other Natural History titles see
newhollandpublishers.com and follow ReedNewHolland and NewHollandPublishers on Facebook